Glossary Words: when a word is printed in **bold**, you can look up its meaning in the Glossary on page 31.

# INTRODUCTION

The core of any armed force is its soldiers, but in the modern battlefield, soldiers are supported by a variety of military machines. These range from troop transporters to mobile heavy artillery. Most of these vehicles incorporate the latest in weapons and armor technology.

### ADVANCING ARMOR
*Tanks have become an integral part of most nations' land forces, combining speed and maneuverability with awesome firepower.*

# HOW TO USE THIS BOOK

## MAIN TEXT
Explains the history of the vehicle and outlines its primary role. Other information, such as which military forces use it, is also covered here.

## SPECIFICATIONS
Gives information about the vehicle's speed, dimensions, and operational range.

## INTERESTING FEATURES
Contains a detailed illustration of the engine or a design feature that makes the vehicle unique. Informative text explains the feature's function.

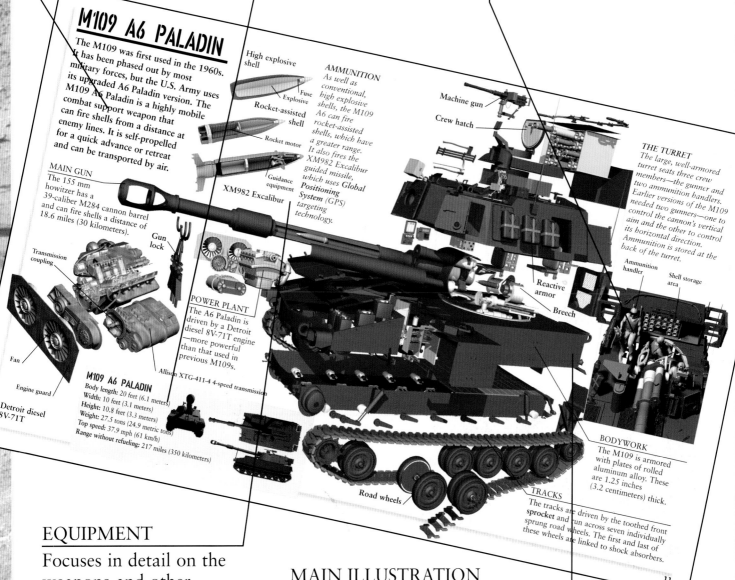

### M109 A6 PALADIN
The M109 was first used in the 1960s. It has been phased out by most military forces, but the U.S. Army uses its upgraded A6 Paladin version. The M109 A6 Paladin is a highly mobile combat support weapon that can fire shells from a distance at enemy lines. It is self-propelled for a quick advance or retreat and can be transported by air.

**MAIN GUN**
The 155 mm howitzer has a 39-caliber M284 cannon barrel and can fire shells a distance of 18.6 miles (30 kilometers).

Gun lock

Transmission coupling

**POWER PLANT**
The A6 Paladin is driven by a Detroit diesel 8V-71T engine —more powerful than that used in previous M109s.

Fan

Engine guard

Detroit diesel 8V-71T

Allison XTG-411-4 4-speed transmission

**M109 A6 PALADIN**
Body length: 20 feet (6.1 meters)
Width: 10 feet (3.1 meters)
Height: 10.8 feet (3.3 meters)
Weight: 27.5 tons (24.9 metric tons)
Top speed: 37.9 mph (61 km/h)
Range without refueling: 217 miles (350 kilometers)

10

High explosive shell

Fuse

Explosive

Rocket-assisted shell

Rocket motor

Guidance equipment

XM982 Excalibur

**AMMUNITION**
As well as conventional, high explosive shells, the M109 A6 can fire rocket-assisted shells, which have a greater range. It also fires the XM982 Excalibur guided missile, which uses Global Positioning System (GPS) targeting technology.

Machine gun

Crew hatch

**THE TURRET**
The large, well-armored turret seats three crew members—the gunner and two ammunition handlers. Earlier versions of the M109 needed two gunners—one to control the cannon's vertical aim and the other to control its horizontal direction. Ammunition is stored at the back of the turret.

Reactive armor

Breech

Ammunition handler

Shell storage area

**BODYWORK**
The M109 is armored with plates of rolled aluminum alloy. These are 1.25 inches (3.2 centimeters) thick.

Road wheels

**TRACKS**
The tracks are driven by the toothed front sprocket and run across seven individually sprung road wheels. The first and last of these wheels are linked to shock absorbers.

11

## EQUIPMENT
Focuses in detail on the weapons and other equipment carried by the vehicle to perform different duties.

## MAIN ILLUSTRATION
Shows the internal structure of the vehicle and gives information on the positions of its various working parts.

# MOBILE ARMOR

**T**he history of armored motorized vehicles dates back to World War I. That conflict witnessed the introduction of the tank—a vehicle that changed the way wars were fought forever.

*BRITISH MARK VI TANK*
*British forces were the first to use tanks. Developed, surprisingly, by the British Royal Navy, they were initially known as "landships."*

## DEVIL'S CHARIOTS

Tanks quickly earned a scary reputation. Although slow and bulky, they were virtually impossible to destroy. **Caterpillar tracks** enabled them to span trenches and smash through barbed wire, while offering **infantry men** a moving shield from enemy fire. By the end of World War I more than six thousand tanks had been built.

*GERMAN A7V TANK*

*ARMORED CAR*
*Vehicles like this were used early in World War I, before the start of warfare from fixed trench lines.*

*RENAULT FT-17*
*Introduced in 1917, this was the first with a fully rotating **turret**.*

## LIGHT TANKS

Smaller and faster than the first tanks, these were pioneered mainly by the French, who made more tanks than anyone else in World War I.

## LIGHTNING WAR

Having proved their usefulness in World War I, tanks were a feature of World War II from its beginning. Germany took the lead in the design and development of tanks.

**GERMAN SD KFZ 250 APC**

*PANZER IV*
*This was the only German tank to be produced all through World War II.*

## HEAVY DUTY

First built to tackle foot soldiers, tanks were now designed to fight one another and so their firepower and armor were increased. World War II also saw the introduction of other military vehicles, such as armored personnel carriers.

*SHERMAN TANK*
*This was the main tank used by U.S. forces in World War II.*

*T-34*
*This Russian all-purpose tank was so effective in World War II that it remained in use until 1996.*

*THE JEEP*
*Lightweight and fast, the jeep was widely used by U.S. forces in World War II and later conflicts.*

# MULTI-ROLE VEHICLES

**S**ome military vehicles are specialized for one purpose, but others can perform a variety of roles. Since World War II, old designs have been improved and new designs have been introduced.

*SOVIET PT-76 LIGHT TANK*
*Introduced in the early 1950s, this tank was **amphibious**, enabling it to cross large rivers.*

*M47 PATTON*
*This U.S. tank entered service in 1952 and continued in use until the late 1980s.*

## COLD WAR STEEL

During World War II, Soviet forces fought alongside the Allies against German troops. Not long after the war ended, a split between the Soviet Union and Western powers appeared and started to grow. This cold war drove the development of new military vehicles by both sides.

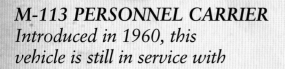

*M-113 PERSONNEL CARRIER*
*Introduced in 1960, this vehicle is still in service with the U.S. Army today.*

*SOVIET T-72*

## TROOP MOVERS

There were significant improvements in the design of tanks, and other types of vehicles also appeared. Among them were armored troop carriers, designed to take **infantry** to the battlefront while shielding them from fire.

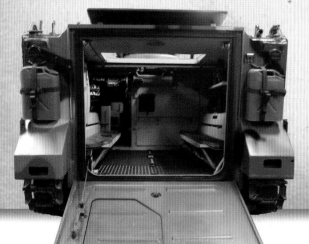

8

### FRENCH VAB APC
*This vehicle is fully amphibious, driven in the water by two water jets on either side of the rear of the hull.*

## WATER-BORNE
Another development was the appearance of military hovercraft and other amphibious vehicles. They could operate in water and on land, crossing muddy land or carrying troops from sea to shore and then across the country.

1960s BELL MILITARY HOVERCRAFT

U.S. AMPHIBIOUS ASSAULT VEHICLE

## COMPLEX MACHINES
Today's military vehicles make use of the greatest mechanical engineering technology. They are well-armed and armored, and fast, with onboard computer systems to aid targeting and navigation on the battlefield.

### LEOPARD 2
*This is the main battle tank of the German Army. It is also used by other countries.*

FV510 WARRIOR INFANTRY SECTION VEHICLE

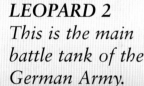

# M109 A6 PALADIN

The M109 was first used in the 1960s. It has been phased out by most military forces, but the U.S. Army uses its upgraded A6 Paladin version. The M109 A6 Paladin is a highly mobile combat support weapon that can fire shells from a distance at enemy lines. It is self-propelled for a quick advance or retreat and can be transported by air.

High explosive shell

Fuse

Explosive

Rocket-assisted shell

Rocket motor

Guidance equipment

**XM982 Excalibur**

*AMMUNITION*
*As well as conventional, high explosive shells, the M109 A6 can fire rocket-assisted shells, which have a greater range. It also fires the XM982 Excalibur guided missile, which uses Global Positioning System (GPS) targeting technology.*

## MAIN GUN

The 155 mm howitzer has a 39-caliber M284 cannon barrel and can fire shells a distance of 18.6 miles (30 kilometers).

Gun lock

Transmission coupling

## POWER PLANT

The A6 Paladin is driven by a Detroit diesel 8V-71T engine —more powerful than that used in previous M109s.

Allison XTG-411-4 4-speed transmission

Fan

Engine guard

Detroit diesel 8V-71T

### M109 A6 PALADIN

**Body length:** 20 feet (6.1 meters)
**Width:** 10 feet (3.1 meters)
**Height:** 10.8 feet (3.3 meters)
**Weight:** 27.5 tons (24.9 metric tons)
**Top speed:** 37.9 mph (61 km/h)
**Range without refueling:** 217 miles (350 kilometers)

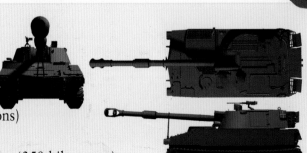

Machine gun

Crew hatch

**THE TURRET**
*The large, well-armored turret seats three crew members—the gunner and two ammunition handlers. Earlier versions of the M109 needed two gunners—one to control the cannon's vertical aim and the other to control its horizontal direction. Ammunition is stored at the back of the turret.*

Ammunition handler

Shell storage area

Reactive armor

Breech

BODYWORK

The M109 is armored with plates of rolled aluminum alloy. These are 1.25 inches (3.2 centimeters) thick.

TRACKS

The tracks are driven by the toothed front **sprocket** and run across seven individually sprung road wheels. The first and last of these wheels are linked to shock absorbers.

Road wheels

# ABRAMS M1A2 MAIN BATTLE TANK

The M1 has been the world's number one tank since 1980. It is fast, mobile, and quiet, and is used by the U.S. Army and Marines. It is named in honor of General Creighton Abrams, former Army chief of staff. Its quiet engine and awesome firepower have led crews to nickname it "The Beast," "Dracula," and "Whispering Death."

## M1A2 ABRAMS

Body length: 25.9 feet (7.9 meters)
Width: 11.8 feet (3.6 meters)
Height to turret: 7.87 feet (2.4 meters)
Weight: 67.6 tons (61.3 metric tons)
Top speed: 42 mph (67.7 km/h)
Range without refueling: 279 miles (450 kilometers)

## GUN

The M256 120 mm **smoothbore** cannon is 17 feet (5.2 meters) long and weighs 2,866 pounds (1.3 tons).

## DRIVER'S STATION

The driver sits in the front and can see outside the tank by using a **periscope**.

Coaxial machine gun

## AMMUNITION

*The main gun fires a variety of ammunition, including high explosive anti-tank (HEAT) and sabot rounds. Sabot rounds do not explode but pierce the armor of enemy tanks.*

HEAT round

Barrel

Penetrator

Sabot round

## MAIN ARMOR

The M1A2 has "Chobham armor," developed in the United Kingdom. It is formed from layers of steel alloy, plastics, ceramics, and **kevlar**.

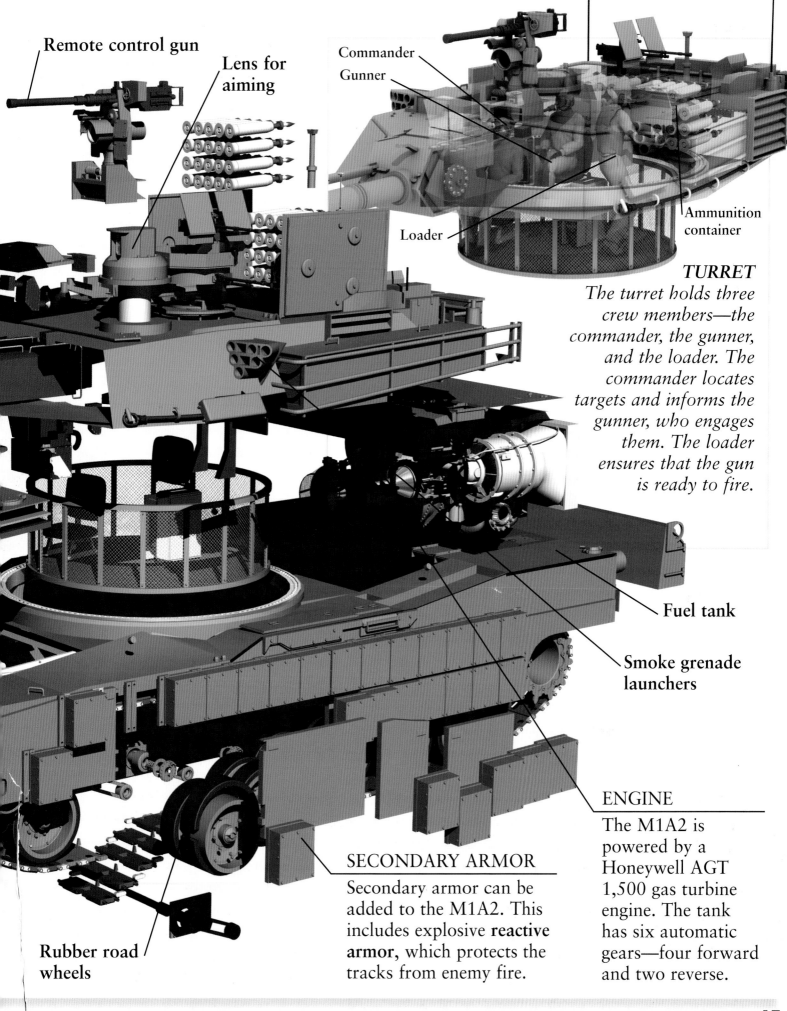

Remote control gun

Lens for aiming

Commander

Gunner

Loader

Ammunition container

**TURRET**
*The turret holds three crew members—the commander, the gunner, and the loader. The commander locates targets and informs the gunner, who engages them. The loader ensures that the gun is ready to fire.*

Fuel tank

Smoke grenade launchers

ENGINE
The M1A2 is powered by a Honeywell AGT 1,500 gas turbine engine. The tank has six automatic gears—four forward and two reverse.

SECONDARY ARMOR
Secondary armor can be added to the M1A2. This includes explosive **reactive armor,** which protects the tracks from enemy fire.

Rubber road wheels

# M270 MULTIPLE ROCKET LAUNCHER

The M270 Multiple Rocket Launcher was jointly developed by the United States, United Kingdom, Germany, and France. It first went into service in 1983 and production ended in 2003, after about 1,300 units had been built. The M270 can fire up to twelve rockets in less than a minute, then move at full speed to avoid returning enemy fire.

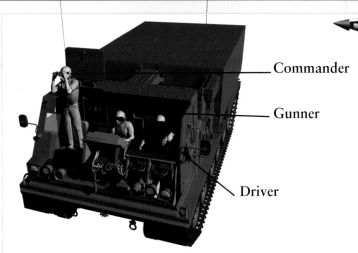

— Commander

— Gunner

— Driver

## CREW COMPARTMENT
*The M270 has a crew of three, who sit up front when the rocket launcher is on the move. The crew compartment is lightly armored to give some protection against small-arms fire.*

## ELECTRONICS
The fire control system has been upgraded since production of the M270 first began. The latest upgrades include a GPS and local wind speed detection technology.

Blast shielding

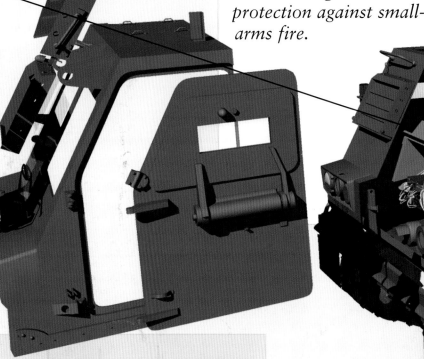

## M270 MLRS
Body length: 22.6 feet (6.9 meters)
Width: 9.6 feet (2.95 meters)
Height: 8.5 feet (2.6 meters)
Weight (loaded): 27.5 tons (24.9 metric tons)
Top speed: 39.7 mph (64 km/h)
Range without refueling: 298 miles (480 kilometers)

## CHASSIS
The **chassis** is based on the M2 Bradley IFV. Like the M2, the M270 is as light as possible for maximized speed.

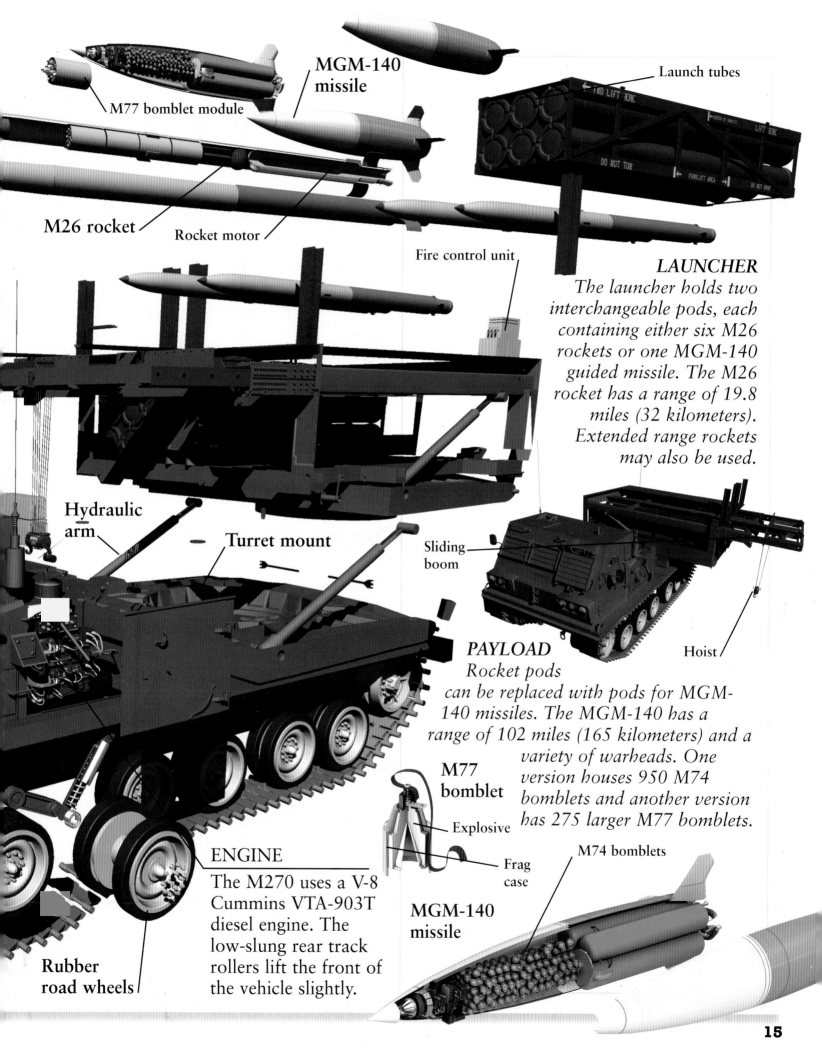

M77 bomblet module

MGM-140 missile

Launch tubes

M26 rocket

Rocket motor

Fire control unit

**LAUNCHER**
*The launcher holds two interchangeable pods, each containing either six M26 rockets or one MGM-140 guided missile. The M26 rocket has a range of 19.8 miles (32 kilometers). Extended range rockets may also be used.*

Hydraulic arm

Turret mount

Sliding boom

Hoist

**PAYLOAD**
*Rocket pods can be replaced with pods for MGM-140 missiles. The MGM-140 has a range of 102 miles (165 kilometers) and a variety of warheads. One version houses 950 M74 bomblets and another version has 275 larger M77 bomblets.*

M77 bomblet

Explosive

Frag case

M74 bomblets

**ENGINE**
The M270 uses a V-8 Cummins VTA-903T diesel engine. The low-slung rear track rollers lift the front of the vehicle slightly.

Rubber road wheels

MGM-140 missile

# M2 BRADLEY IFV

The M2 Bradley Infantry Fighting Vehicle (IFV) is an armored infantry transporter. It takes troops onto the battlefield and provides covering fire. Using its Tube-launched, Optically tracked, Wire-guided (TOW) missile launcher, it can also destroy tanks. It was developed for the U.S. Army to complement the Abrams M1 tank and was introduced in 1981.

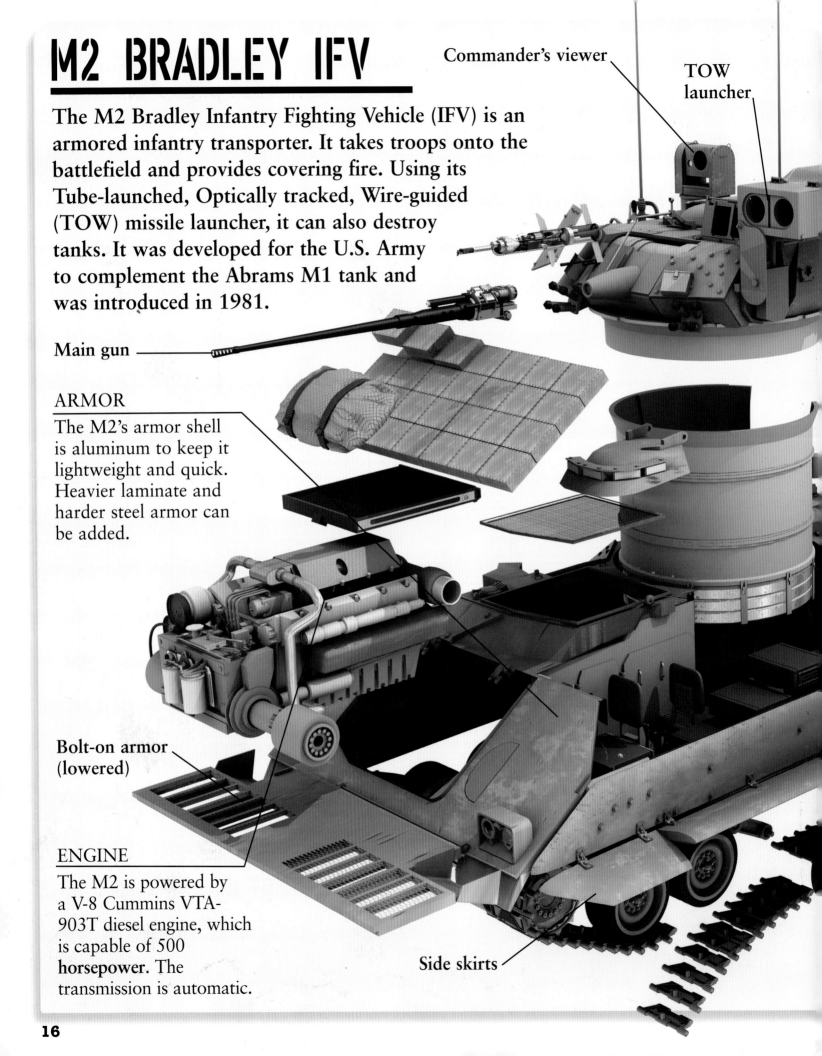

Commander's viewer

TOW launcher

Main gun

## ARMOR

The M2's armor shell is aluminum to keep it lightweight and quick. Heavier laminate and harder steel armor can be added.

Bolt-on armor (lowered)

## ENGINE

The M2 is powered by a V-8 Cummins VTA-903T diesel engine, which is capable of 500 **horsepower**. The transmission is automatic.

Side skirts

## TURRET

**Gunner's station**

*This houses the M2's commander and gunner. Hatches allow the soldier to stand up with their upper body outside the tank, but during combat these hatches are closed. The turret is armed with a 25 mm M242 chain gun and a twin tube TOW anti-tank missile launcher. The TOW launcher is used when the M2 is stationary.*

M242 chain gun

Gunner

## M2 BRADLEY INFANTRY FIGHTING VEHICLE

Body length: 21.9 feet (6.7 meters)
Width: 10.8 feet (3.3 meters)
Height: 9.8 feet (3 meters)
Weight: 24.8 tons (22.5 metric tons)
Top speed: 41 mph (66 km/h)
Range without refueling:
300 miles (483 kilometers)

Warhead

TOW missile

Extendable probe

## TROOP COMPARTMENT

This seats up to six fully armed soldiers. Troops enter and exit through the armored rear door, which is hinged at the bottom.

Loading the TOW launcher

Display screen

Rear door

Reactive armor

Infantryman

## WHEELS AND TRACKS

The track is driven by the front sprocket. Behind this are six dual rubber-tire road wheels. The track itself has replaceable rubber pads for use on paved roads.

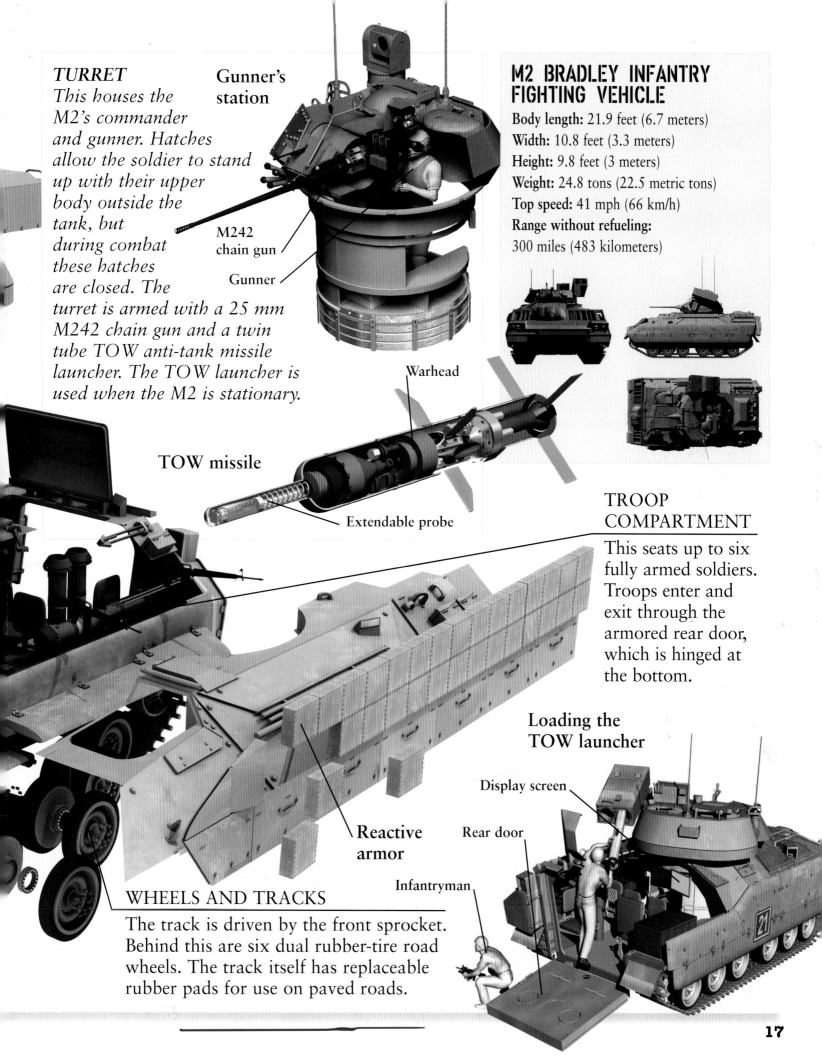

# BV 206S ALL-TERRAIN CARRIER

The Bandvagn (BV) 206 is an all-terrain carrier with caterpillar tracks that tows a separate trailer that can move independently. It was developed for the Swedish Army and went into production in 1981. Today, the BV 206 is operated by many armed forces, including the U.S. and British armies. The BV 206S is an armored version.

## BODYWORK

The bodywork of the standard BV 206 is fire-resistant, glass-reinforced plastic. The BV 206S has additional steel armor and bulletproof glass.

## DRIVER'S STATION

The driver sits in the front unit, which can also seat three passengers. The unit is insulated with PVC foam.

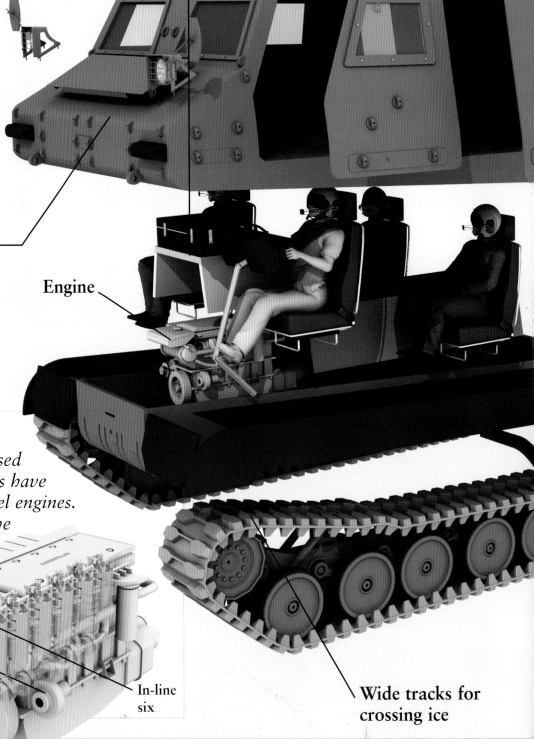

Engine

## ENGINE

*The first BV 206 vehicles used gas engines, but new models have Mercedes-Benz 136 hp diesel engines. The engine is mounted in the front unit and drives all four tracks.*

Turbocharger

Mercedes-Benz OM603.950 diesel engine

In-line six

Wide tracks for crossing ice

## TRAILER

The troop-carrying trailer has space for eleven soldiers but can be adapted for carrying troops or cargo. Other variants include a mortar carrier and an antitank gun platform.

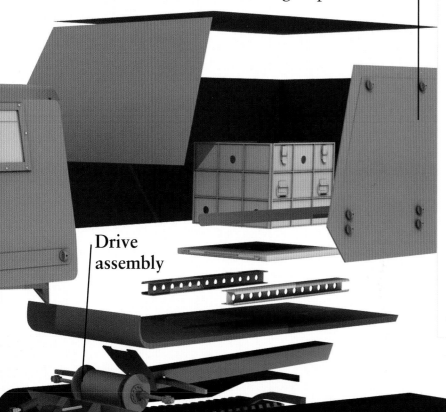

**Drive assembly**

## ARTILLERY HUNTING RADAR

*The ARTillery HUnting Radar (ARTHUR) system can be mounted on the trailer of the BV 206. ARTHUR uses* **microwaves** *to detect the positions and types of enemy guns. Response fire can then be rapidly coordinated and tracked from the trailer by the radar controllers.*

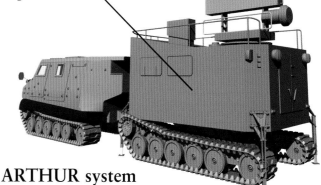

Radar

Operators' cab

**ARTHUR system**

Track mount

## WHEELS AND TRACKS

The tracks are made of molded, reinforced rubber, unique to the BV 206. They are driven by the front-mounted sprocket, which is raised above wheel level.

## LINKAGE

The linkage contains a steering unit, but is flexible, so the vehicle can easily move across rough terrain.

**Powered articulated linkage**

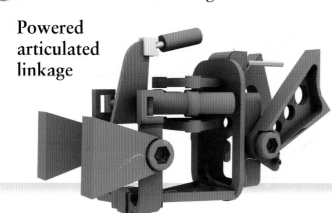

## BANDVAGN 206S

Total length: 22.6 feet (6.9 meters)
Width: 6.2 feet (1.9 meters)
Height: 7.8 feet (2.4 meters)
Weight: 7.7 tons (7.7 metric tons)
Top speed: 31 mph (50 km/h)
Range without refueling: 205 miles (330 kilometers)

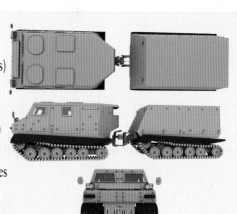

# HMMWV HUMVEE

The HMMWV (High-Mobility Multipurpose Wheeled Vehicle), or Humvee, is a lightweight, four-wheel drive vehicle with automatic gears. It was designed for the U.S. Army and introduced in 1985. It has been adapted to serve many functions, from field ambulance to missile launching platform.

## HMMWV HUMVEE

**Length:** 15 feet (4.6 meters)
**Width:** 7.2 feet (2.2 meters)
**Height:** 5.9 feet (1.8 meters), reducible to 4.5 feet (1.4 meters)
**Weight:** 2.6 tons (2.3 metric tons)
**Top speed:** 65 mph (105 km/h)
**Range without refueling:**
349 miles
(563 kilometers)

## BODYWORK

The standard HMMWV body is relatively lightweight, to improve its all-terrain capabilities. Additional armor is added to some models, for protection against mines and light arms.

GEP Optimizer
6500 V-8

*ENGINE*
*The HMMWV is powered by a 6.2 or 6.5 liter fuel-injected V-8 diesel engine, capable of reaching up to 200 horsepower. It has automatic gears with four forward and one reverse gear.*

Fan

Cylinders

Gearbox

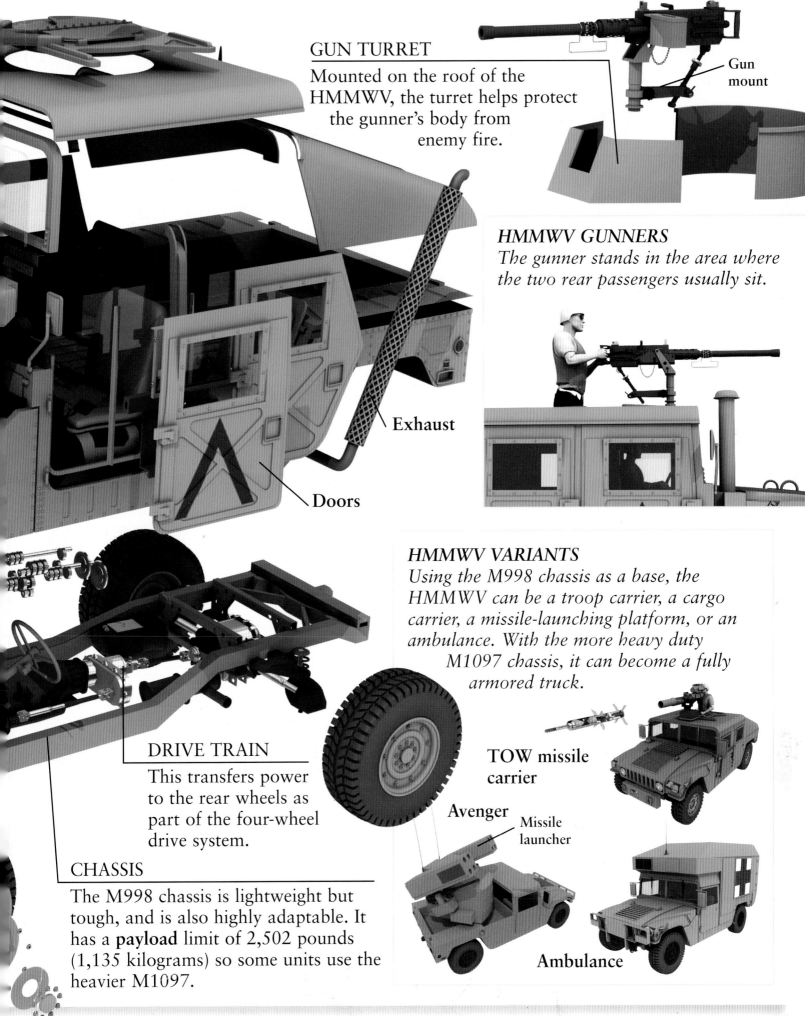

## GUN TURRET

Mounted on the roof of the HMMWV, the turret helps protect the gunner's body from enemy fire.

Gun mount

*Exhaust*

*Doors*

### HMMWV GUNNERS

*The gunner stands in the area where the two rear passengers usually sit.*

### HMMWV VARIANTS

*Using the M998 chassis as a base, the HMMWV can be a troop carrier, a cargo carrier, a missile-launching platform, or an ambulance. With the more heavy duty M1097 chassis, it can become a fully armored truck.*

TOW missile carrier

Avenger

Missile launcher

## DRIVE TRAIN

This transfers power to the rear wheels as part of the four-wheel drive system.

## CHASSIS

The M998 chassis is lightweight but tough, and is also highly adaptable. It has a **payload** limit of 2,502 pounds (1,135 kilograms) so some units use the heavier M1097.

Ambulance

# LCAC MILITARY HOVERCRAFT

The Landing Craft Air Cushion (LCAC) military hovercraft is a high-speed vehicle used for transporting tanks, troops, or equipment from the deck of a warship to the top of a beach. First deployed in 1987, it is used by the U.S. Navy and the Japan Maritime Self-Defense Force.

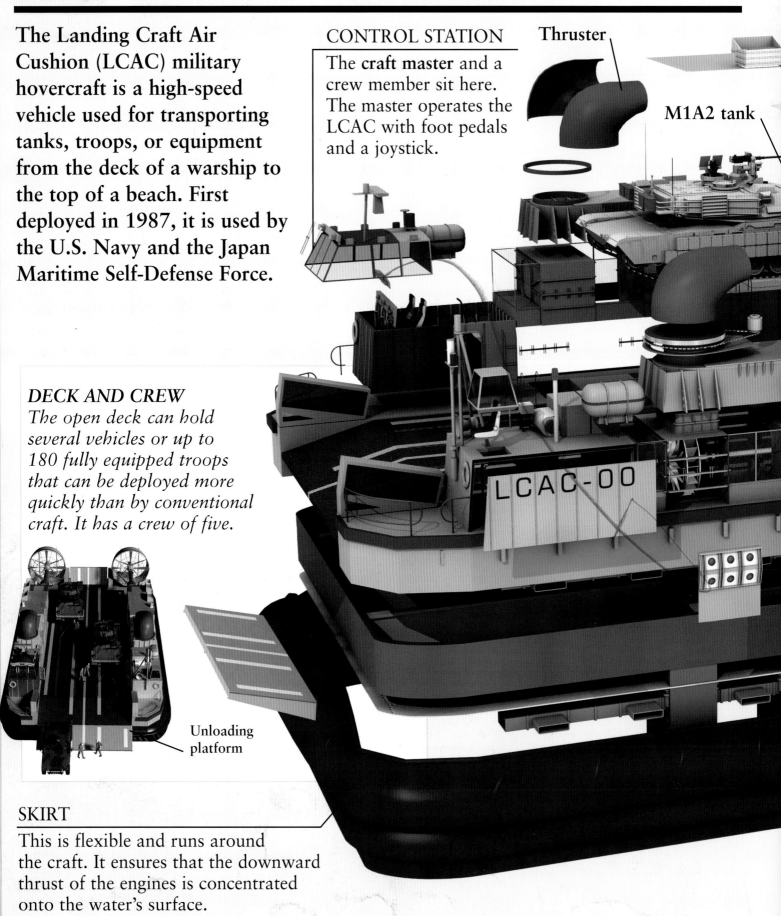

### CONTROL STATION

The **craft master** and a crew member sit here. The master operates the LCAC with foot pedals and a joystick.

**Thruster**

**M1A2 tank**

### DECK AND CREW

*The open deck can hold several vehicles or up to 180 fully equipped troops that can be deployed more quickly than by conventional craft. It has a crew of five.*

Unloading platform

### SKIRT

This is flexible and runs around the craft. It ensures that the downward thrust of the engines is concentrated onto the water's surface.

## ENGINES AND PROPELLERS

The LCAC has four TF-40B gas turbine engines—two for lift and two for propulsion. In many older units the engines have been replaced with ETF-40B gas turbines.

**TF-40B gas turbine**

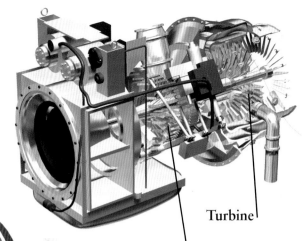

Turbine

Compressor unit

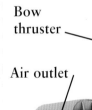

R345 propeller

US NAVY

*LIFT FANS*
*These generate the downward flow of air needed to lift the LCAC up and off the water or land. Once up and running, the fans hold the hovercraft 5.9 feet (1.8 meters) above the surface.*

Bow thruster

Air outlet

Downward thrust units

## LANDING CRAFT AIR CUSHION

**Length:** 86.6 feet (26.4 meters)
**Width:** 46.9 feet (14.3 meters)
**Top speed:** 46 mph (74 km/h)
**Maximum load:** 75 tons (68 metric tons)
**Range without refueling:**
300 miles
(483 kilometers)
**Crew:** 5

# M1126 STRYKER

The M1126 Stryker Infantry Carrier Vehicle (ICV) is an armored personnel transporter. It carries soldiers into the battle zone and provides covering fire for them as they dismount and take up their positions. It was first deployed in Iraq in 2003 and is used exclusively by the U.S. Army.

Belt feed

M151 remote weapons station

Smoke grenade launchers

Video lens for aiming

## WEAPONS
*The M1126 carries an M151 remote weapons station that features an M2 Browning .50 caliber machine gun, and can be aimed, moved, and fired by an operator inside.*

Driver's hatch

## ENGINE

The M1126 uses a C7 diesel engine. This engine is used in several other U.S. Army vehicles, which makes running repairs easier.

Driver's station

## SUSPENSION

Each of the eight wheels has independent **hydro-pneumatic suspension**. The suspension can be adjusted to lift the vehicle higher off the ground.

Drive unit

## WHEELS AND TIRES

An internally controlled system alters the pressure in all eight tires to suit terrain conditions. It can also alert the driver to a flat tire.

## ARMOR

The armor is hard steel with lightweight ceramic layers. Inside the vehicle there is an automatic fire extinguishing system.

## M1126 STRYKER TROOP COMPARTMENT

This has space for up to nine battle ready infantry troops. The M1126 also has two crew members, and the driver and commander, who stay with the vehicle.

### STRYKER M1126

**Length:** 22.9 feet (7 meters)
**Width:** 8.8 feet (2.7 meters)
**Height:** 8.8 feet (2.6 meters)
**Weight:** 18.1 tons (16.4 metric tons)
**Top speed:** 60 mph (97 km/h)
**Range without refueling:** 329 miles (531 kilometers)

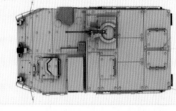

M68A1 rifled cannon

### M1128 MOBILE GUN SYSTEM

*Unlike the M1126, which uses a M151 remote weapons station, the M1128 has a 105 mm tank cannon, as well as space for ammunition and a gun operator. The M1128 is designed to offer heavy supporting fire to infantry troops on the ground.*

# MRAP-COUGAR HE

The MRAP-Cougar was introduced into service in 2002. It protects its occupants from mines, small arms fire, and improvised explosive devices (IEDs), such as roadside bombs. It has seen action in Iraq and Afghanistan. It is used by U.S., Canadian, British, Iraqi, Italian, and Polish forces.

### Cougar encounters a roadside IED

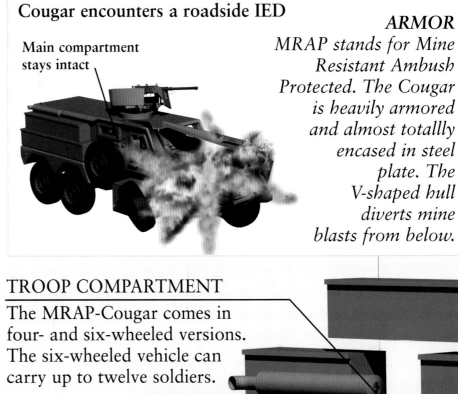

Main compartment stays intact

*ARMOR*
*MRAP stands for Mine Resistant Ambush Protected. The Cougar is heavily armored and almost totallly encased in steel plate. The V-shaped hull diverts mine blasts from below.*

## MRAP-COUGAR HE

Length: 24.6 feet (7.5 meters)
Width: 8.8 feet (2.7 meters)
Height: 9.8 feet (3 meters)
Weight: 19.5 tons (19.1 metric tons)
Top speed: 55 mph (88 km/h)
Range without refueling: 420 miles (676 kilometers)

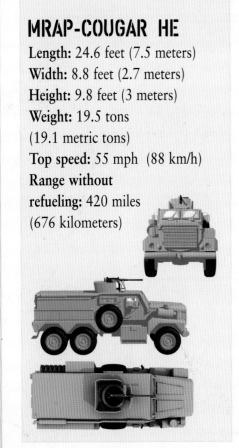

## TROOP COMPARTMENT

The MRAP-Cougar comes in four- and six-wheeled versions. The six-wheeled vehicle can carry up to twelve soldiers.

Storage lockers

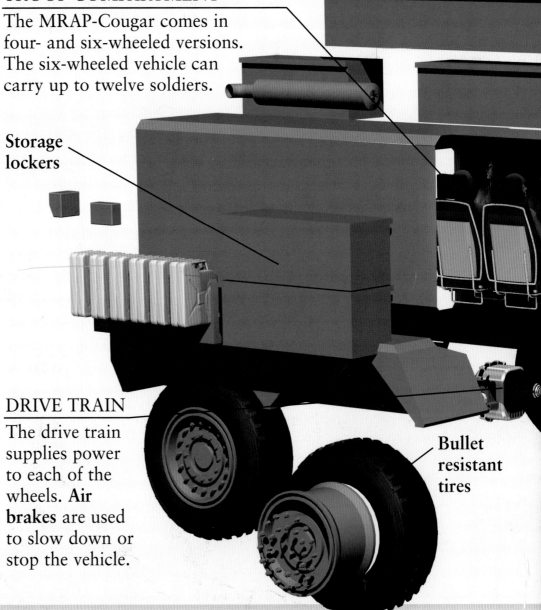

## DRIVE TRAIN

The drive train supplies power to each of the wheels. **Air brakes** are used to slow down or stop the vehicle.

Bullet resistant tires

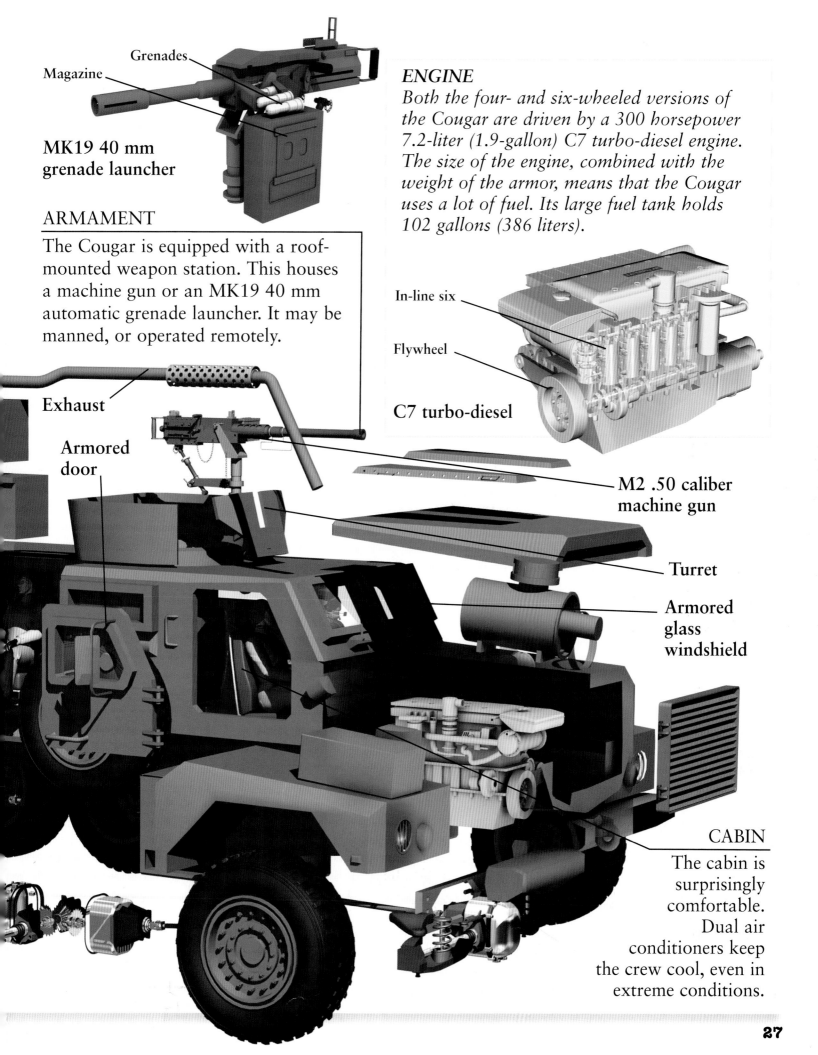

Magazine
Grenades

**MK19 40 mm grenade launcher**

## ARMAMENT

The Cougar is equipped with a roof-mounted weapon station. This houses a machine gun or an MK19 40 mm automatic grenade launcher. It may be manned, or operated remotely.

## ENGINE

*Both the four- and six-wheeled versions of the Cougar are driven by a 300 horsepower 7.2-liter (1.9-gallon) C7 turbo-diesel engine. The size of the engine, combined with the weight of the armor, means that the Cougar uses a lot of fuel. Its large fuel tank holds 102 gallons (386 liters).*

In-line six

Flywheel

**C7 turbo-diesel**

Exhaust

Armored door

**M2 .50 caliber machine gun**

Turret

Armored glass windshield

## CABIN

The cabin is surprisingly comfortable. Dual air conditioners keep the crew cool, even in extreme conditions.

# EXPEDITIONARY FIGHTING VEHICLE

The Expeditionary Fighting Vehicle (EFV) is the latest amphibious vehicle to be designed for the U.S. Marine Corps. Part landing craft and part tank, it is due to be deployed in 2015. The EFV will transport marines from ships to land and then directly into battle. It is highly mobile on land and faster than an M1 tank.

## TURRET
*Manned by a single gunner, the turret can fire on other vehicles and provide covering fire for marines disembarking from the unit.*

Main gun

Vision blocks

Lens for aiming

## EFV
**Length:** 35.1 feet (10.7 meters)
**Width:** 12.1 feet (3.7 meters)
**Height:** 10.8 feet (3.3 meters)
**Weight:** 37.3 tons (33.8 metric tons)
**Top speed:** 28.5 mph (46 km/h) (land), 44 mph (72 km/h) (water)

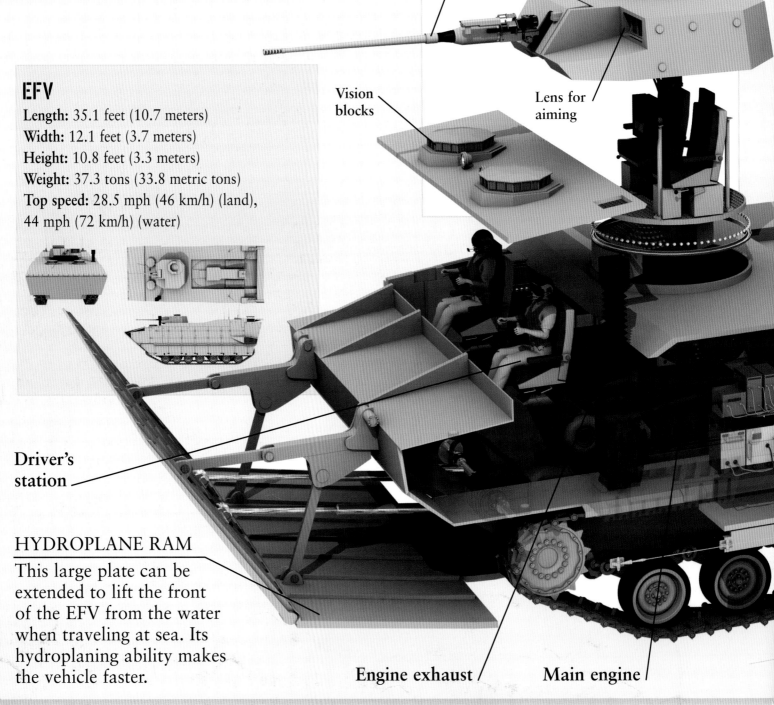

Driver's station

## HYDROPLANE RAM
This large plate can be extended to lift the front of the EFV from the water when traveling at sea. Its hydroplaning ability makes the vehicle faster.

Engine exhaust

Main engine

## TROOP COMPARTMENT

This houses seventeen fully equipped and combat-ready Marines. Its walls are heavily armored.

## ARMOR

The hull of the EFV is made from aluminum with mine-blast protection. The rest is covered with composite armor (consisting of layers of different material).

## *ENGINE*

*The EFV is driven by a single MT 883 Ka-523 twelve cylinder diesel engine. This engine has two modes of operation—a high power mode, used for driving the vehicle at sea, and a low power mode, which is used on land. In high power mode the engine reaches 2,702 horsepower.*

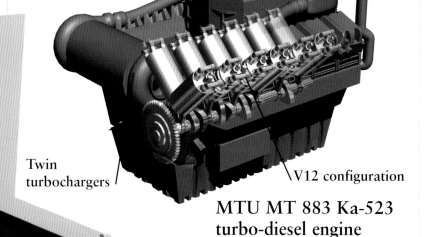

Twin turbochargers

V12 configuration

**MTU MT 883 Ka-523 turbo-diesel engine**

## PROPULSION SYSTEMS

At sea, the EFV is launched by water-jet propulsion, which is built into either side of the hull. On land, transmission switches to the vehicle's tracks, which are covered when the EFV is in water.

## GUN

The main armament of the EFV is mounted as part of the turret. It fires two hundred rounds per minute and can destroy lightly armored vehicles and aircraft, as well as enemy personnel.

**Bushmaster II 30 mm chain gun**

Recoil spring

# FUTURE MACHINES

Military technology constantly advances and vehicles are regularly replaced by new models designed to perform most effectively in the ever-changing arenas of war.

Design programs aim to improve both military assault and protection systems. Developing unmanned vehicles is one way of reducing the risk to fighting troops. The Armed Robotic Vehicle (ARV) is a five ton (4.5 metric ton) unmanned ground vehicle with either assault or reconnaissance capabilities. Reducing energy consumption is also a priority so research is focusing on hybrid-electric technology for more efficient, powerful, and versatile machines.

## UPGRADES
*To save costs some machines are refitted with the latest equipment or redesigned. This BMP-1 is upgraded with a remotely operated turret.*

## FUTURE COMBAT SYSTEMS
*The Future Combat Systems (FCS) Non-Line-Of-Sight Gun are beginning to replace the M109 self-propelled howitzers, which are currently used by the U.S. Army.*

## ARMED ROBOTIC VEHICLE
*Armed unmanned vehicles are becoming a reality. The FCS ARV has an advanced suspension system and can venture where it is too dangerous for foot soldiers to go.*

# GLOSSARY

**air brakes**
Brakes that use compressed air to push brake pads to slow the wheels down.

**amphibious**
Able to operate both on land and in the water.

**caterpillar tracks**
A moving track made up of many metal links. The tank's engine rotates sprockets, which move the track, and the tank's wheels ride along the track.

**chassis**
The rectangular steel frame that forms the skeleton of a motor vehicle. The axles and the frame that support the bodywork are attached to the chassis.

**craft master**
The captain or commanding officer of a hovercraft.

**Global Positioning System (GPS)**
A system of satellites that allows people with specialized receivers to pinpoint exactly where they are on the Earth.

**heavy artillery**
Large caliber weapons that need a crew to operate them, firing from the ground at other surface targets.

**horsepower**
The amount of power transferred from a vehicle's engine to its wheels or tracks.

**hydro-pneumatic suspension**
Suspension that uses pneumatic springs filled with fluid, rather than coiled metal ones. Pneumatic springs use pressurized gas—air or wind.

**infantryman**
A soldier who fights on foot.

**kevlar**
A light, extremely strong, synthetic fiber.

**microwaves**
A short electromagnetic wave.

**payload**
The weight of people and material that a vehicle can carry.

**periscope**
An instrument containing lenses and mirrors that allows the viewer an unobstructed view on all sides.

**reactive armor**
Defensive armor attached to the outside of a tank that reacts in some way to the impact of a shell. Explosive reactive armor contains small explosive charges that detonate when hit, helping to counteract and force away the impact of a shell.

**sabot round**
A bullet, shell, or other round that is surrounded by a casing to increase its diameter, so it can be fired from large bore weapons. As the round leaves the barrel, its casing falls away.

**smoothbore**
A barrel with a hole that has no grooves.

**sprocket**
A toothed wheel.

**turret**
A revolving structure on a vehicle that protects the gunner and revolves to let the weapon be aimed in many directions.

# INDEX